I0425891

March 2012

2011 LOBBYING DISCLOSURE

Observations on Lobbyists' Compliance with Disclosure Requirements

GAO

Accountability ★ Integrity ★ Reliability

2011 LOBBYING DISCLOSURE

Observations on Lobbyists' Compliance with Disclosure Requirements

Highlights of GAO-12-492, a report to congressional committees

Why GAO Did This Study

HLOGA requires lobbyists to file quarterly lobbying disclosure reports and semiannual reports on certain political contributions. HLOGA also requires that GAO annually (1) determine the extent to which lobbyists can demonstrate compliance with disclosure requirements, (2) identify any challenges to compliance that lobbyists report, and (3) describe the resources and authorities available to the Office and the efforts the Office has made to improve its enforcement of the LDA. This is GAO's fifth report under the mandate. GAO reviewed a stratified random sample of 100 quarterly LD-2 reports filed for the third and fourth quarters of calendar year 2010 and the first and second quarters of calendar year 2011. GAO also reviewed two random samples totaling 160 LD-203 reports from year-end 2010 and midyear 2011. This methodology allowed GAO to generalize to the population of 51,792 disclosure reports with $5,000 or more in lobbying activity and 32,301 reports of federal political campaign contributions. GAO also met with officials from the Office regarding efforts to focus resources on lobbyists who fail to comply. GAO provided a draft of this report to the Attorney General for review and comment. The Assistant U.S. Attorney for the District of Columbia responded on behalf of the Attorney General that the Department of Justice had no comments on the draft of this report.

View GAO-12-492. For more information, contact J. Christopher Mihm at (202) 512-6806 or mihmj@gao.gov.

What GAO Found

Most lobbyists were able to provide documentation to demonstrate compliance with disclosure requirements. This finding is similar to GAO's results from prior reviews. There are no specific requirements for lobbyists to create or maintain documentation related to disclosure reports they file under the Lobbying Disclosure Act of 1995 as amended (LDA). Nonetheless, and similar to last year's results, for two key elements of the reports (income and expenses), GAO estimates that lobbyists could provide documentation to support approximately 93 percent of the disclosure reports for the third and fourth quarters of 2010 and the first and second quarters of 2011. According to documentation lobbyists provided for income and expenses, GAO estimates that the amounts disclosed were properly reported and supported for 63 percent of the quarterly lobbying disclosure (LD-2) reports. For lobbyists and lobbying firms listed on the LD-2 report, an estimated 86 percent filed year-end 2010 or midyear 2011 reports of federal political campaign contributions (LD-203) reports as required. For LD-203 political contributions reports, GAO estimates that a minimum of 4 percent of all LD-203 reports omitted one or more reportable political contributions that were documented in the Federal Election Commission database. Fewer lobbyists—17 this year versus 21 in the prior year—stated that they planned to amend their LD-2 report following GAO's reviews to make correction on one or more data elements. As of March 2012, 9 of 17 amended their disclosure reports.

Lobbyists are required to file LD-2 reports for the quarter in which they first register. The majority of lobbyists who newly registered with the Secretary of the Senate and Clerk of the House of Representatives in the third and fourth quarters of 2010 and first and second quarters of 2011 filed required disclosure reports for that period. GAO could identify corresponding reports on file for lobbying activity for 88 percent of registrants.

The majority of lobbyists felt that the terms associated with disclosure reporting were clear and understandable and the requirements were easy to meet. However, a few lobbyists reported challenges in complying with the LDA.

The U.S. Attorney's Office for the District of Columbia (the Office) stated that it has resources and authorities to pursue civil or criminal cases for noncompliance with LDA requirements. To enhance enforcement efforts and support the 17 staff who have been working on compliance issues on a part-time basis, the Office hired one contract staff member in September 2010 who works full-time on lobbying compliance issues. The Office has primarily focused on contacting lobbyists who have potentially violated the LDA by not filing disclosure reports. In November 2011, the Office settled its first enforcement case since the enactment of the Honest Leadership and Open Government Act of 2007 (HLOGA), and reached a $45,000 settlement with a lobbying firm that had been referred to the Office repeatedly for failure to file disclosure reports. More than half of the 561 lobbyists who were contacted for noncompliance with LD-2 requirements for calendar years 2009 and 2010 are now compliant. Approximately 1,081 lobbyists were referred by the Secretary of the Senate for noncompliance with LD-203 requirements for calendar year 2009.

_____ United States Government Accountability Office

Contents

Figures

Abbreviations

Clerk of the House	Clerk of the House of Representatives
DOJ	Department of Justice
FEC	Federal Election Commission
HLOGA	Honest Leadership and Open Government Act of 2007
LDA	Lobbying Disclosure Act of 1995
Office	U.S. Attorney's Office for the District of Columbia

United States Government Accountability Office
Washington, DC 20548

March 30, 2012

Congressional Committees

Questions regarding the influence of special interests in the formation of government policy have led to a move toward more transparency and accountability with regard to the lobbying community. The Honest Leadership and Open Government Act of 2007 (HLOGA)[1] amended the Lobbying Disclosure Act of 1995 (LDA)[2] to require lobbyists to file quarterly lobbying disclosure reports and semiannual reports on certain political contributions. HLOGA also increased civil penalties and added criminal penalties for failure to comply with LDA requirements. The mandate requires GAO to audit the extent of lobbyists' compliance with the requirements of the LDA by reviewing publicly available lobbying registrations and a random sampling of reports filed during each calendar year.[3] Our report shall include any recommendations related to improving lobbyists' compliance with the LDA and information on resources and authorities available to the U.S. Attorney's Office for the District of Columbia (the Office) for effective enforcement of the LDA. This is our fifth mandated review of lobbyists' disclosure reports filed under the LDA.

Consistent with our mandate, our objectives were to (1) determine the extent to which lobbyists can demonstrate compliance with the LDA, as amended, by providing documentation to support information contained in reports filed under the LDA, (2) identify any challenges that lobbyists report to compliance and potential improvements, and (3) describe the resources and authorities available to the Office in its role in enforcing compliance with the LDA and the efforts the Office has made to improve its enforcement of the LDA.

To fulfill our audit requirement in HLOGA, we took the following steps:

To determine the extent to which lobbyists can demonstrate compliance, we selected a stratified random sample of 100 quarterly lobbying

---

[1] Pub. L. No. 110-81, 121 Stat. 735 (Sept. 14, 2007).

[2] Pub. L. No. 104-65, 109 Stat. 691 (Dec. 19, 1995) (2 U.S.C. §§ 1601-1614).

[3] 2 U.S.C. § 1614.

GAO-12-492 2011 Lobbying Disclosure

disclosure (LD-2) reports with income and expenses of $5,000 or more filed during the third and fourth quarters of calendar year 2010 and the first and second quarters of calendar year 2011.[4] We selected the randomly sampled reports from the publicly downloadable database maintained by the Clerk of the House of Representatives (Clerk of the House). Appendix II contains a list of lobbyists (registrants and clients) who we randomly selected for our review of LD-2 reports. This methodology allows us to generalize to the population of these LD-2 reports. We then contacted each lobbyist or lobbying firm[5] in our sample and asked them to provide supporting documentation for key elements of their LD-2 reports, including the amount of money received for lobbying activities, the houses of Congress or executive branch agencies lobbied, lobbying issue areas, and lobbyists reported as having worked on the issues. We also reviewed whether lobbyists listed on the LD-2 reports properly disclosed prior covered official positions, and whether the lobbyists filed the semiannual report of federal political contributions. All lobbyists in our sample responded to our requests for supporting documentation.

To determine whether lobbyists' reported their federal political contributions as required by the LDA, we analyzed stratified random samples of year-end 2010 and midyear 2011 semiannual federal political contributions (LD-203) reports. The samples contain 80 LD-203 reports that have contributions listed and 80 LD-203 reports that list no contributions. We selected the randomly sampled reports from the publicly downloadable contributions database maintained by the Clerk of the House. See appendix III for a list of lobbyists and lobbying firms randomly selected for our review of LD-203 reports. We then checked the

---

[4] LD-2 reports for third quarter 2010 are from the prior review and are included in the current review to redistribute the LD-2 reports evenly across the calendar year for this and future lobbying reviews. This will allow us enough time to complete reviews and conduct the analysis of the data prior to our required reporting date. For the prior report, GAO-11-452, we drew a sample from the fourth quarter of calendar year 2009 and the first, second, and third quarters of calendar year 2010. See GAO, *2010 Lobbying Disclosure: Observations on Lobbyists' Compliance with Disclosure Requirements*, GAO-11-452 (Washington, D.C.: Apr. 1, 2011).

[5] Although we contacted each lobbyist or lobbying firm in our sample, we did not always meet with the lobbyists identified as the point of contact or the actual lobbyists, we met with individuals representing lobbyists or lobbying firms. For the purposes of this review, we use the term lobbyists to refer to lobbyists, lobbying firms, and individuals representing the lobbyists that were present during the review.

contributions reported in the Federal Election Commission's (FEC) database against the contributions identified in our sample to determine whether all contributions reported in the FEC database were also reported on the LD-203s, as required. We contacted lobbyists and asked them to provide documentation to clarify differences we observed. All lobbyists complied with our request to provide documentation. This methodology allows us to generalize to the population of LD-203 reports both with and without contributions.

To determine whether registrants were meeting the requirement to file an LD-2 report for the quarter in which they registered, we compared new registrations (commonly referred to as LD-1s) filed in the third and fourth quarters of 2010 and the first and second quarters of 2011 to the corresponding LD-2 reports on file with the Clerk of the House.

To identify challenges and potential improvements to compliance, we used structured interviews to obtain views from lobbyists included in our sample of reports.

To describe the resources and authorities available to the Office and efforts the Office has made to improve its enforcement of the LDA, we interviewed officials from the Office and obtained information on the level of staffing and resources dedicated to the enforcement of the LDA, and the practices they have established to enforce the LDA. The Office provided us with information on the processes used to enforce compliance with the LDA and reports from the tracking system on the number and status of referrals.

The mandate does not require GAO to identify lobbyist organizations that failed to register and report in accordance with LDA requirements. The mandate also does not require us to determine whether reported lobbying activity or contributions represented the full extent of lobbying activities that took place.

We conducted this performance audit from June 2011 to March 2012 in accordance with generally accepted government auditing standards. Those standards require that we plan and perform the audit to obtain sufficient, appropriate evidence to provide a reasonable basis for our findings and conclusions based on our audit objectives. We believe that the evidence obtained provides a reasonable basis for our findings and conclusions based on our audit objectives. For more details on our methodology, see appendix I.

Background

The LDA, as amended by HLOGA, requires lobbyists to register with the Secretary of the Senate and the Clerk of the House and file quarterly reports disclosing their lobbying activity. Lobbyists are required to file their registrations and reports electronically with the Secretary of the Senate and the Clerk of the House through a single entry point (as opposed to separately with the Secretary of the Senate and the Clerk of the House as was done prior to HLOGA). Registrations and reports must be publicly available in downloadable, searchable databases from the Secretary of the Senate and the Clerk of the House. No specific requirements exist for lobbyists to generate or maintain documentation in support of the information disclosed in the reports they file. However, guidance issued by the Secretary of the Senate and the Clerk of the House recommends that lobbyists retain copies of their filings and supporting documentation for at least 6 years after they file their reports.

The LDA requires that the Secretary of the Senate and the Clerk of the House provide guidance and assistance on the registration and reporting requirements of the LDA and develop common standards, rules, and procedures for compliance with the LDA. The Secretary and the Clerk review the guidance semiannually. The guidance was last revised and published in December 2011. The guidance provides definitions of terms in the LDA, elaborates on the registration and reporting requirements, includes specific examples of different scenarios, and provides explanations of why certain scenarios prompt or do not prompt disclosure under the LDA. In meetings with the Secretary of the Senate and Clerk of the House, they stated that they consider information we report on lobbying disclosure compliance when they periodically update the guidance.

The LDA defines a lobbyist as an individual who is employed or retained by a client for compensation, who has made more than one lobbying contact (written or oral communication to a covered executive or legislative branch official made on behalf of a client), and whose lobbying activities[6] represent at least 20 percent of the time that he or she spends on behalf of the client during the quarter.[7] Lobbying firms are persons or

---

[6] Lobbying activities include not only direct lobbying contacts but also efforts in support of such contacts, such as preparation and planning activities, research, and other background work that is intended for use in contacts.

[7] 2 U.S.C. § 1602(10)

entities that have one or more employees who lobby on behalf of a client other than that person or entity.[8]

Lobbying firms are required to file a registration with the Secretary of the Senate and the Clerk of the House for each client if the firms receive or expect to receive over $3,000 in income or $11,500 in incurred expenses from that client for lobbying activities.[9] Lobbyists are also required to submit a quarterly report, also known as an LD-2 report, for each registration filed. The registration and subsequent LD-2 reports contain the following elements, if applicable:

- the name of the organization, lobbying firm, or self-employed individual that is lobbying on that client's behalf;
- a list of individuals who acted as lobbyists on behalf of the client during the reporting period;
- whether any lobbyists served as covered executive branch or legislative branch officials "covered officials" in the previous 20 years;[10]
- the name of and further information about the client, including a general description of its business or activities;
- information on the specific lobbying issue areas and corresponding general issue codes used to describe lobbying activities;
- any foreign entities that have an interest in the client;
- whether the client is a state or local government;

---

[8] 2 U.S.C. § 1602(9).

[9] Organizations employing in-house lobbyists file only one registration. An organization is exempt from filing if total expenses in connection with lobbying activities are not expected to exceed $11,500. Amounts are adjusted for inflation and published in the LDA guidance.

[10] The LDA defines a covered executive branch official as the President, Vice President, an officer or employee, or any other individual functioning in the capacity of such an officer or employee of the Executive Office of the President; an officer or employee serving in levels I through V of the Executive Schedule; members of the uniformed services whose pay grade is at or above O-7; and any officer or employee serving in a position of a confidential, policy-determining, policymaking, or policy-advocating character who is excepted from competitive service as determined by the Office of Personnel Management (commonly called Schedule C employees). The LDA defines a covered legislative branch official as a member of Congress, an elected officer of either house of Congress, or any employee or any other individual functioning in the capacity of an employee of a member, a committee of either House of Congress, the leadership staff of either House of Congress, a joint committee of Congress, or a working group or caucus organized to provide legislative services or other assistance to members. 2 U.S.C. § 1602(3), (4).

- information on which federal agencies and House(s) of Congress the lobbyist contacted on behalf of the client during the reporting period;
- the amount of income related to lobbying activities received from the client (or expenses for organizations with in-house lobbyists) during the quarter rounded to the nearest $10,000; and
- a list of constituent organizations that contribute more than $5,000 for lobbying in a quarter and actively participate in planning, supervising, or controlling lobbying activities, if the client is a coalition or association.

The LDA, as amended, also requires lobbyists to report certain contributions semiannually in the LD-203 report. These reports must be filed 30 days after the end of a semiannual period by each lobbying firm registered to lobby and by each individual listed as a lobbyist on a firm's lobbying reports. The lobbyists or lobbying firms must

- list the name of each federal candidate or officeholder, leadership political action committee, or political party committee to which they made contributions equal to or exceeding $200 in the aggregate during the semiannual period;
- report contributions made to presidential library foundations and presidential inaugural committees;
- report funds contributed to pay the cost of an event to honor or recognize a covered official, funds paid to an entity named for or controlled by a covered official, and contributions to a person or entity in recognition of an official or to pay the costs of a meeting or other event held by or in the name of a covered official; and
- certify that they have read and are familiar with the gift and travel rules of the Senate and House and that they have not provided, requested, or directed a gift or travel to a member, officer, or employee of Congress that would violate those rules.

The Secretary of the Senate and the Clerk of the House, along with the Office are responsible for ensuring compliance with the LDA. The Secretary of the Senate and the Clerk of the House notify lobbyists or lobbying firms in writing that they are not complying with reporting requirements in the LDA, and subsequently refer those lobbyists who fail to provide an appropriate response to the Office. The Office researches these referrals and sends additional noncompliance notices to the lobbyists, requesting that the lobbyists file reports or correct reported information. If the Office does not receive a response after 60 days, it decides whether to pursue a civil or criminal case against each noncompliant lobbyist. A civil case could lead to penalties up to $200,000, while a criminal case—usually pursued if a lobbyist's noncompliance is found to be knowing and corrupt—could lead to a maximum of 5 years in prison.

Documentation to Support Some LD-2 Report Elements Varied, but Most Newly Registered Lobbyists Met Disclosure Reporting Requirements

Most Lobbyists Provided Documentation for LD-2 Reports, but Documentation for Some Report Elements Did Not Match Their Disclosure Reports

As in our prior reviews, most lobbyists reporting $5,000 or more in income or expenses were able to provide documentation to varying degrees for the reporting elements in their disclosure reports.[11] Lobbyists for an estimated 93 percent of LD-2 reports were able to provide documentation to support the income and expenses reported for the third and fourth quarters of 2010 and the first and second quarters of 2011.[12] Last year, we reported that lobbyists for an estimated 97 percent of LD-2 reports were able to provide documentation for income and expenses for the quarters under review.[13] The most common forms of documentation provided included invoices for income and payroll records for expenses. According to the documentation lobbyists provided for income and

---

[11] See GAO-11-452, and GAO, *2009 Lobbying Disclosure: Observations on Lobbyists' Compliance with Disclosure Requirements*, GAO-10-499 (Washington, D.C.: Apr. 1, 2010); *2008 Lobbying Disclosure: Observations on Lobbyists' Compliance with Disclosure Requirements*, GAO-09-487 (Washington, D.C.: Apr. 1, 2009); and *Lobbying Disclosure: Observations on Lobbyists' Compliance with New Disclosure Requirements*, GAO-08-1099 (Washington, D.C.: Sept. 30, 2008).

[12] Our sample is only one of a large number of samples that we might have drawn. Because each sample could have provided different estimates, we express our confidence in the precision of our estimate as a 95 percent confidence interval. This interval would contain the actual population value for 95 percent of the samples we could have drawn. Unless otherwise stated, all percentage estimates have a maximum 95 percent confidence interval of within 10.0 percentage points or less of the estimate.

[13] GAO-11-452.

expenses, we estimate that the amount disclosed was properly rounded to the nearest $10,000 and supported for 63 percent (59 of 93) of the LD-2 reports; differed by at least $10,000 from the reported amount in 16 percent (15 of 93) of LD-2 reports; and had rounding errors in 21 percent (19 of 93) of LD-2 reports.[14]

Figure 1 illustrates the extent to which lobbyists were able to provide documentation to support selected elements on the LD-2 reports.

Figure 1: Documentation Lobbyists Provided to Support Selected Elements of LD-2 Reports

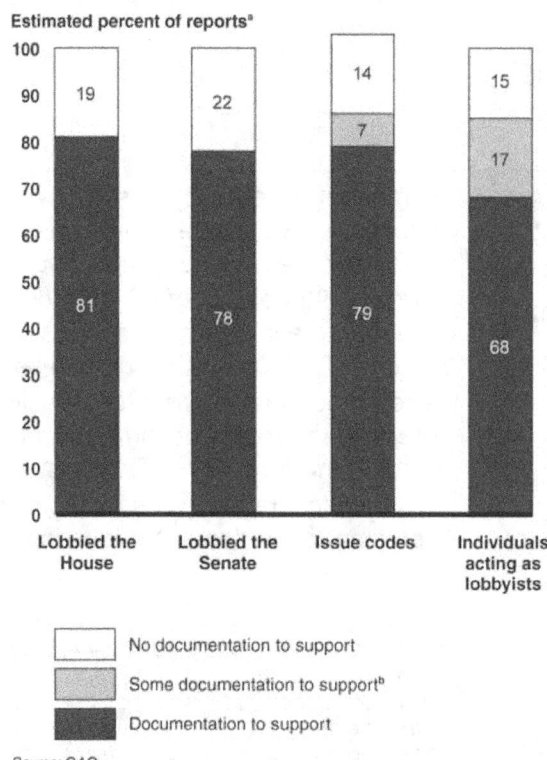

Estimated percent of reports[a]

No documentation to support

Some documentation to support[b]

Documentation to support

Source: GAO.

---

[14] Lobbyists are expected to provide a good faith estimate on the LD-2 report of income and expenses reported rounded to the nearest $10,000. Our estimate of the number of reports with rounding errors includes reports that disclosed the exact amount of income from or expenditures on lobbying activities, but failed to round to the nearest $10,000 as required.

[a]Percentage estimates in the figure have a 95 percent confidence interval of plus or minus 10 percentage points or less of the estimates.

[b]Lobbyists having some documentation to support issue codes and the names of individuals acting as lobbyists refers to the lobbyists being able to provide documentation for only some of the total number of issue codes or lobbyists reported.

Of the 100 LD-2 reports in our sample, 47 disclosed lobbying activities at executive branch agencies, with lobbyists for 19 of these reports providing documentation to support lobbying activities at all agencies listed.

Table 1 lists the common reasons why lobbyists we interviewed said they did not have documentation for some of the elements of their LD-2 reports.

Table 1: Reasons Lobbyists in Our Sample Cited for Not Having Documentation for Some Elements of Their LD-2 Reports

LD-2 report element	Reasons for not having documentation
Lobbied the Houses of Congress	Several lobbyists told us they did not keep documentation of their lobbying contacts with the House and the Senate. Additionally several lobbyists told us they overreported contact with the House and Senate staff and that the contact did not occur during the quarter under review.
Lobbied executive branch agencies	Several lobbyists told us they did not keep documentation of their contacts with executive branch agencies. Several lobbyists told us they overreported their contact with the agencies and that lobbying activity with the agencies listed did not occur during the quarter under review.
Individuals acting as lobbyists	As in last year's report, several lobbyists told us they listed all lobbyists on the LD-2 reports even if they did not lobby on behalf of the client during the quarter under review. Several lobbyists stated that they might have lobbied on behalf of the client in a previous quarter but not the quarter under review.
Covered positions	Several lobbyists told us it was oversight that they did not disclose the covered positions and that they planned to amend their LD-2 reports. Confusion still exists among some lobbyists as to whether congressional interns were considered covered positions and therefore need to be disclosed.[a]

Source: GAO.

[a]In our last report, officials from the Offices of the Secretary of the Senate and Clerk of the House confirmed that internships are considered covered official positions and therefore should be disclosed.

Most Lobbyists Properly Disclosed Covered Positions as Required

The LDA requires a lobbyist to disclose previously held covered positions when first registering as a lobbyist for a new client, either on the LD-1 or on the LD-2 quarterly filing when added as a new lobbyist. Based on our analysis, we estimate that a minimum of 11 percent of all LD-2 reports did not properly disclose one or more previously held covered positions.[15] This finding is consistent with last year's report.[16] Lobbyists for an estimated 86 percent of LD-2 reports filed year-end 2010 or midyear 2011 LD-203 contribution reports for all of the lobbyists and lobbying firms listed on the report as required.[17] All individual lobbyists and lobbying firms reporting specific lobbying activity are required to file LD-203 reports semiannually, even if they have no contributions to report, because they must certify compliance with the gift and travel rules.

Fewer Lobbying Firms Indicated That They Planned to Amend Their LD-2 Reports as a Result of GAO's Review

Compared to our last review, fewer lobbying firms indicated that they plan to amend their LD-2 reports as a result of our review. This year, lobbying firms for 17 of the LD-2 reports in our sample indicated that they planned to amend their LD-2 reports as a result of our review. Last year, 21 lobbying firms indicated they planned to amend their LD-2 reports. As of March 2012, 9 lobbying firms have amended their LD-2 reports (compared to 12 lobbying firms last year).

Specific reasons for filing amendments included the following:

- Decreasing reported income from $60,000 to $30,000
- Increasing the reported income from $20,000 to $30,000
- Changing the client's name on the LD-2 report
- Adding additional information about the specific issues lobbied
- Adding contact with the House
- Removing reported contact with the Senate
- Adding a federal agency
- Adding covered positions
- Adding a lobbyist

---

[15] For information on our methodology, see app. I.

[16] GAO-11-452.

[17] As part of our LD-2 report review, we checked the Clerk of the House's database to ensure that each lobbyist and organization listed on the LD-2 report filed an LD-203 report during the most recent reporting period.

In addition, lobbying firms filed amendments for 3 (compared to 8 reports last year)[18] of the LD-2 reports in our sample after being notified that their LD-2 reports were selected as part of our random sample but prior to our review.

Some LD-203 Contribution Reports Omitted Political Contributions Listed in the FEC Database

We estimate that overall, a minimum of 4 percent of reports failed to disclose one or more contributions.[19] As part of our review, we compared contributions listed on lobbyists' and lobbying firms' LD-203 reports against those political contributions reported in the FEC database to identify whether political contributions were omitted on LD-2 reports in our sample. The sample of LD-203 reports we reviewed contained 80 reports with political contributions and 80 reports without political contributions. Of the 80 LD-203 reports sampled with contributions reported, 12 reports omitted one or more contributions. Of the 80 LD-203 reports sampled with no contributions reported, 2 reports failed to disclose contributions listed in the FEC database.

Most Newly Registered Lobbyists Filed Disclosure Reports as Required

Of the 3,802 new registrations we identified from fiscal year 2011, we were able to match 3,357 reports filed in the first quarter in which they were registered. This is a match rate of 88 percent of registrations, which is consistent with our prior reviews.[20] To determine whether new registrants were meeting the requirement to file, we matched newly filed registrations in the third and fourth quarters of 2010 and the first and second quarters of 2011 from the House Lobbyist Disclosure Database to their corresponding quarterly disclosure reports using an electronic matching algorithm that allows for misspelling and other minor inconsistencies between the registrations and reports.

---

[18] GAO-11-452.

[19] We did not estimate the percentage of other non-FEC political contributions that were omitted (such as honoraria or gifts to presidential libraries) because they tend to constitute a small minority of all listed contributions and cannot be verified against an external data source.

[20] GAO-11-452 and GAO-10-499.

While Most Lobbying Firms Reported That the Disclosure Requirements Were Easy or Somewhat Easy to Meet, a Few Lobbyists Reported Challenges in Complying with the Act

Disclosure Requirements Were Easy or Somewhat Easy to Meet for Most Lobbying Firms

As part of our review, 90 different lobbying firms were included in our sample.[21] Of the 90 lobbying firms, 86 reported that the disclosure requirements were "easy" or "somewhat easy" to meet.[22] Of the 86 lobbying firms in our sample of LD-2 reports that said the requirements were "easy" or "somewhat easy" to meet, 61 lobbyists indicated that the requirements were "easy" and 25 indicated that the requirements were "somewhat easy" to meet. Compared to last year, fewer lobbyists told us that they found the quarterly reporting requirement difficult to meet. This year, 5 lobbyists we interviewed (compared to 10 lobbyists last year)[23] said that it was difficult to file reports quarterly or difficult to meet the 20 day filing deadline. The deadline for filing disclosure reports is 20 days

---

[21] The number of lobbying firms total 90 and is less than our sample of 100 reports because some lobbying firms had more than one LD-2 report included in our sample for lobbyists that we interviewed on the same day. In these cases, we interviewed each lobbyist once to ask about lobbying disclosure requirements and the clarity of lobbying terms.

[22] Although the quantitative results from lobbyists in our sample of LD-2 reports are generalizable to all LD-2 reports, the qualitative results are not generalizable because our sample was designed to develop population estimates of the accuracy of information on LD-2 reports and was not designed to estimate the opinions of lobbyists.

[23] GAO-11-452.

after each reporting period, or the first business day after the 20th day if the 20th day is not a business day.[24]

A Few Lobbyists Cited Challenges in Complying with the Act

While most lobbyists we interviewed told us they thought that the terms associated with LD-2 reporting requirements were clear, a few lobbyists highlighted areas of confusion in applying some aspects of LDA reporting requirements. This is consistent with our prior report. We asked the lobbyists we interviewed to rate various terms associated with LD-2 reporting as being "clear and understandable," "somewhat clear and understandable," or, "not clear and understandable." Figure 2 shows the terms associated with LD-2 reporting that the lobbyists were asked to rate and how they responded to each term. Table 2 summarizes the feedback we obtained from the lobbying firms in our sample of reports that rated the lobbying terms as either "not clear and understandable" or "somewhat clear and understandable."

---

[24] Prior to the enactment of HLOGA, the deadline for filing disclosure reports was 45 days after the end of each reporting period.

Figure 2: Rating of Terms Associated with LD-2 Reporting for Lobbyists in Interviews

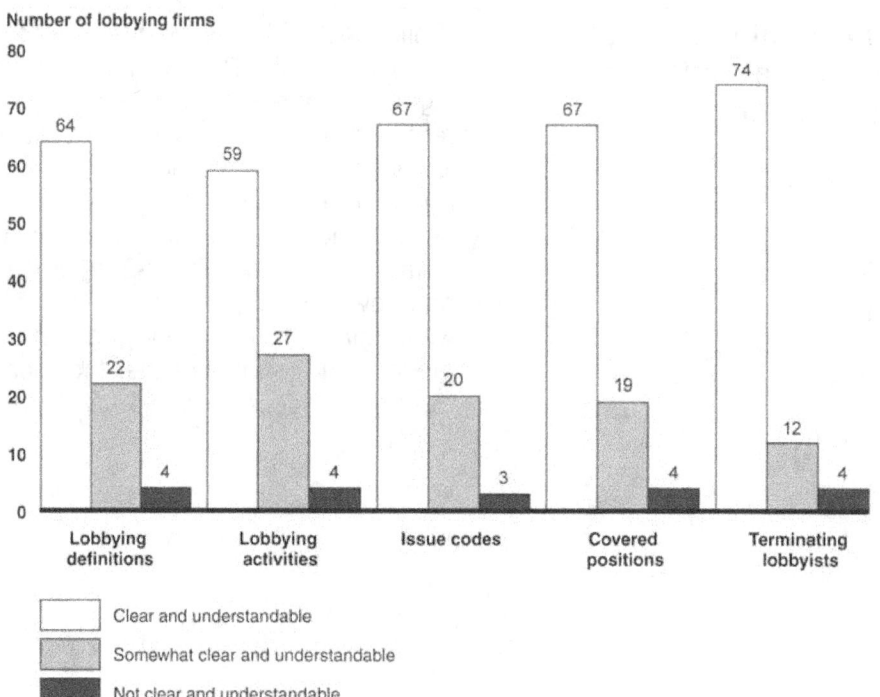

Number of lobbying firms

Clear and understandable

Somewhat clear and understandable

Not clear and understandable

Source: GAO.

Table 2: Feedback from Lobbyists in Our Sample of Reports Who Rated the Lobbying Terms as Either "Not Clear and Understandable" or "Somewhat Clear and Understandable"

Associated terms	Feedback about LD-2 terminology and challenges to reporting
Lobbying definitions	Some lobbyists stated that lobbying definitions were unclear and that it was difficult to determine which activities met the definition of lobbying activity. A few lobbyists said that it was difficult to understand the definition of lobbying activities or determine whether 20 percent of their time over the three-month period was spent on lobbying activities.
Lobbying activities	Some lobbyists still expressed concern about differentiating between lobbying activities versus nonlobbying activities. For example, some lobbyists said they were not sure when research and support activities become lobbying activities and therefore needed to be disclosed.[a]
Issue codes	Some lobbyists said additional clarity would be helpful to determine the most appropriate issue codes to use. For example, lobbyists mentioned confusion with using an appropriation code versus the specific issue area code.
Covered positions	Some lobbyists continued to express concern about knowing when a federal official they met with held a covered position. Some lobbyists said they might overreport their meetings because they are unclear whether the person they met with held a covered position.
Terminating lobbyists	Few lobbyists expressed concerns about when to terminate a lobbyist who was no longer lobbying on behalf of the client.

Source: GAO.

[a]The LDA guidance provides examples of lobbying activities, which includes preparation or planning activities and research and background work that is expected to be used in contacting and coordinating the lobbying activities of others.

U.S. Attorney's Office Actions to Enforce the LDA

The Office's Authorities, Processes, and Resources to Enforce LDA Compliance

The Office stated that it has sufficient resources and authority to enforce compliance with LDA requirements, including imposing civil or criminal penalties for noncompliance. In a prior report, we recommended that the Office develop a structured approach for the tracking and recording of enforcement activities for lobbyists whom the Secretary of the Senate and the Clerk of the House identify as failing to comply with LDA requirements.[25] As a result, the Office developed a system that allowed it to track when referrals are received, record reasons for referrals, record actions taken to resolve them, and assess the results of actions taken. The system has allowed the Office to take actions to achieve compliance with the LDA. The Office uses the summary reports to track progress and quickly identify lobbyists that continuously fail to comply. In addition, the Office hired one contract staff member in September 2010 to work on lobbying compliance issues on a full-time basis. This has enhanced the Office's ability to pursue enforcement actions by centralizing the process of checking and resolving referrals. The Office has 17 staff to assist with lobbying compliance issues on a part-time basis.

To enforce LDA compliance, the Office has primarily focused on sending letters to lobbyists who have potentially violated the LDA by not filing disclosure reports as required. The letters request that lobbyists comply with the law by promptly filing the appropriate disclosure documents. Not all referred lobbyists receive noncompliance letters because some of the lobbyists have terminated their registrations, or lobbyists may have complied by filing the report before the Office sent noncompliance letters. In addition to sending letters, the contractor sends e-mails and calls lobbyists to inform them of their need to comply with the LDA requirements. Figure 3 describes the process and time frames of the Office's enforcement efforts.

---

[25] GAO-08-1099.

Figure 3: U.S. Attorney's Office Process for Addressing Referrals Received from the Secretary of the Senate and Clerk of the House

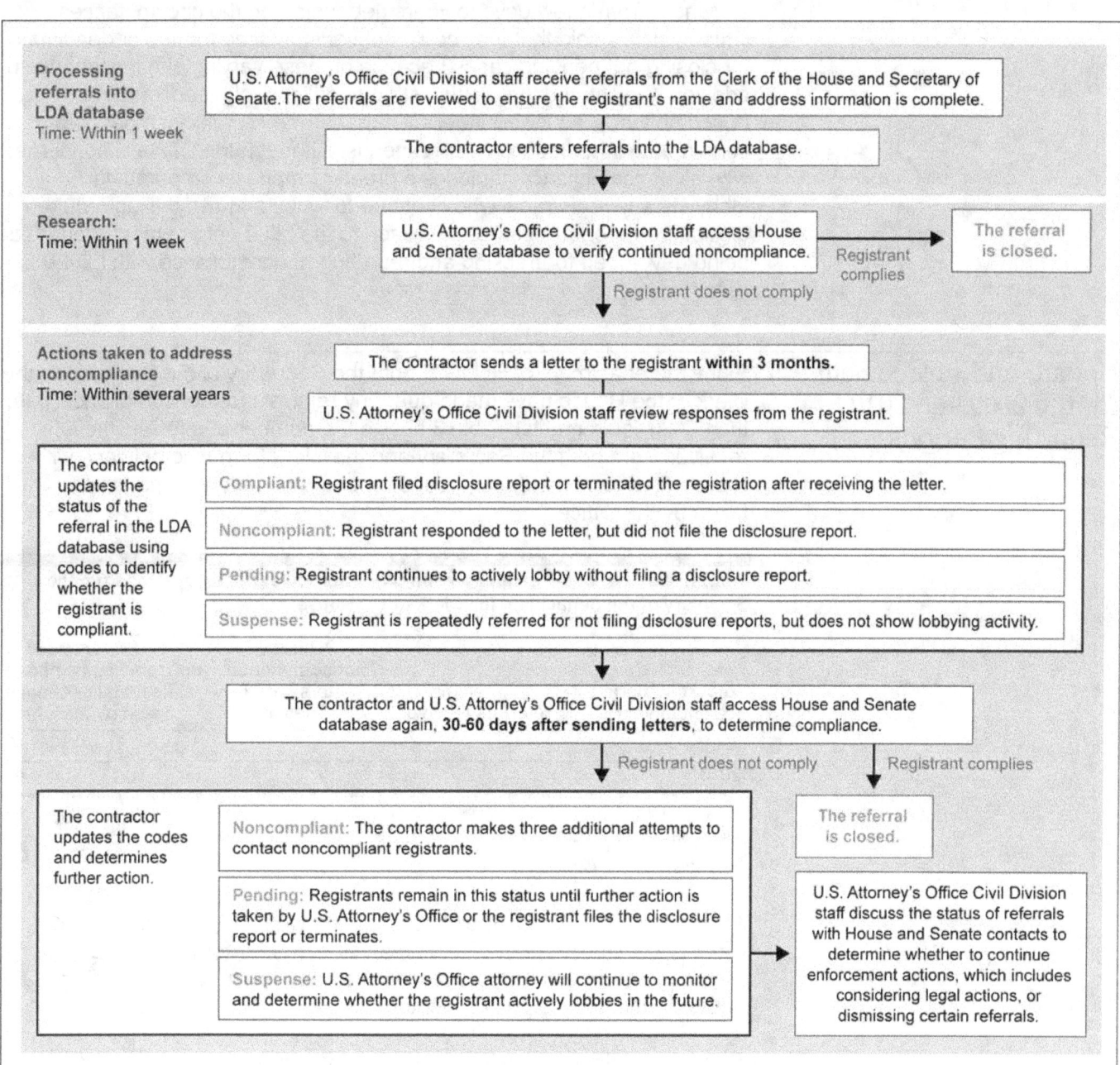

Source: U.S. Attorney's Office for the District of Columbia.

Typically, lobbyists resolve their noncompliance issues by filing the reports or terminating their registration. Resolving referrals can take anywhere from a few days to years depending on the circumstances. Office officials said that they could not set strict time frames or deadlines for closing out pending cases because of these varying circumstances. In addition, they stated that setting strict deadlines might encourage noncompliance if a lobbyist believes that a referral will close out on a certain date if he or she never responds. Although the Office is concerned with all noncompliance, it places a greater emphasis on pursuing lobbyists and registrants who continue to lobby and avoid filing required disclosure reports. A similar approach to the LD-2 enforcement process is being developed for tracking and reporting noncompliance with LD-203 reporting.

Update on Enforcement for the 2009 and 2010 Reporting Periods

Since the enactment of HLOGA, both the Secretary of the Senate and the Clerk of the House have made quarterly referrals for noncompliance with the LD-2 requirements. Table 3 shows the number of referrals the Office received from both the Secretary and the Clerk for noncompliance with reports filed for the 2009 and 2010 reporting periods and the actions taken by the Office.

Table 3: Number of LD-2 Referrals the U.S. Attorney's Office Received from the Secretary of the Senate and the Clerk of the House

Reporting period (calendar year)	Number of referrals received[a]	Number of noncompliance letters sent by the Office[b]	Number of noncompliance phone calls made or e-mails sent by the Office
2009	457	320	0
2010	446	193	48

Source: U.S. Attorney's Office for the District of Columbia.

[a]As of January 25, 2012.

[b]As of February 22, 2012.

As of January 25, 2012, the Office has received 118 referrals from the Clerk of the House for the first and second quarter for the 2011 LD-2 reporting period, but has not yet received any referrals from the Secretary of the Senate for the 2011 reporting period.

As shown in figure 4, about 56 percent (312 of 561) of the lobbyists who received letters, phone calls, or e-mails from the Office for noncompliance for 2009 and 2010 LD-2 referrals have either filed reports or have terminated their registrations and are now considered compliant. Additionally, about 43 percent (243 of 561) are pending action because the Office did not receive a response from the lobbyist and plans to conduct additional research to determine if it can locate the lobbyist. The remaining 1 percent of (6 of 561) referrals did not require action because the lobbyist or client was no longer in business or the lobbyist was deceased. In addition, lobbyists were found to be compliant when the Office received the referral. This may occur when lobbyists have responded to the contact letters from the Secretary of the Senate and Clerk of the House after the Office has received the referrals.

Figure 4: Status of LDA Enforcement Actions for LD-2 Reporting (as of February 22, 2012)

	2009	2010	Total
Total Number of registrants who received phone calls, e-mails or a letter from the U.S. Attorney's Office[a]	320	241	561
Number of referrals now compliant	191	121	312
Number of referrals pending action	125	118	243
Number of referrals with no Action taken by the U.S. Attorney's Office	3	3	6

Source: U.S. Attorney's Office for the District of Columbia.

[a]Letters sent includes those sent to referred registrants who may have been referred for noncompliance with more than one client.

The Office has also received referrals from the Secretary of the Senate and the Clerk of the House for noncompliance with LD-203 reports. The Office sends noncompliance letters to the registered organizations and includes the names of the lobbyists who did not comply with the requirement to report federal campaign and political contributions and certify that they understand the gift rules. For noncompliance in the 2009 filing period, as of January 25, 2012, the Office has received LD-203 referrals from the Secretary of the Senate for 1,081 lobbyists. As of

March 23, 2012, the Office received LD-203 referrals from the Secretary of the Senate for noncompliance in the 2010 filing period and from the Clerk of the House for the 2009 and 2010 filing periods; however, the Office is still processing the referrals. As of February 22, 2012, the Office has mailed 68 noncompliance letters to the registered organizations.[26] The registered organizations may receive a noncompliance letter listing the name of more than one lobbyist. As a result, the number of letters sent will not match the number of referrals now compliant, pending, and with no action taken. However, 7 percent of (73 of 1,081) referrals did not require action because the lobbyist was no longer in business, deceased, or found to be compliant when the Office received the referral. This may occur when lobbyists have responded to the contact letters from the Secretary of the Senate and Clerk of the House after the Office has received the referrals. Table 4 shows the status of enforcement actions for LD-203 reporting after noncompliance letters were sent to registrant organizations for 2009.

Table 4: Status of LDA Enforcement Actions for LD-203 Referrals for the 2009 Filing Period (as of February 22, 2012)

Actions taken for LD-203 referrals for the 2009 filing period	Number of LD-203 referrals
Number of referrals now compliant	97
Number of referrals pending action	530
Number of referrals with no action taken by the Office	73

Source: U.S. Attorney's Office for the District of Columbia.

Status of Pending Enforcement Actions

According to officials from the Office, many of the LD-2 pending cases represent lobbyists who are no longer lobbying or have never filed a disclosure report. Officials from the Office stated that they have been working more closely with the Senate and the House to remove these referrals before they are forwarded to the Office.

The Office has mailed noncompliance letters to the registered organizations and included the names of the lobbyists who did not comply

---

[26] The Office is in the process of updating the noncompliance letter it sends to referred organizations. Officials said that they plan to send the new letters to the remaining referred organizations starting in the fall of 2012.

with the LD-203 requirement. However, Office officials said that there have been complaints within the lobbying community regarding responsibility for responding to letters of noncompliance with LD-203 requirements. They also said that many lobbyists who were not in compliance no longer lobby for the organizations affiliated with the referrals, even though these organizations may be listed on their original lobbyist registration. Organizations are not responsible for an individual lobbyist's failure to comply with the LD-203 disclosure requirement, nor are they required to provide contact information for the noncompliant lobbyist. Because of these limitations, officials told us that the Office has very little leverage to bring individual lobbyists into compliance. Officials stated that many of the LD-203 pending cases remain open in an attempt to locate the individual lobbyists, and as a result, these referrals may take years to resolve.

Enforcement Settlement Actions

Since the enactment of the LDA in 1995, but before the 2008 implementation of HLOGA, the Office had settled with three lobbyists who failed to file and collected civil penalties totaling about $47,000. In November 2011, the Office settled its first enforcement case since the enactment of HLOGA in 2007 and reached a $45,000 settlement with a lobbying firm that had been referred to the Office repeatedly for failure to file disclosure reports. HLOGA increased the penalties for offenses committed after January 1, 2008. As stated earlier, a civil case could lead to penalties up to $200,000, while a criminal case—usually pursued if lobbyists' noncompliance is found to be knowing and corrupt—could lead to a maximum of 5 years in prison.

We previously reported that the Office planned to identify additional cases of repeat LDA noncompliance for civil enforcement review in the spring and summer of 2011. The Office conducted research and used the system it developed to identify and track lobbyists and firms that have a history of chronic noncompliance. As a result, the Office has developed a "top 10 list" of noncompliant lobbyists whom it may potentially pursue for enforcement actions using five civil enforcement attorneys who have been assigned to review the cases.

Agency Comments

We provided a draft of this report to the Attorney General for review and comment. We met with the Assistant U.S. Attorney for the District of Columbia, who on behalf of the Attorney General responded that Department of Justice had no comments of the draft of this report.

We are sending copies of this report to the Attorney General, Secretary of the Senate, Clerk of the House of Representatives, and interested congressional committees and members. In addition, this report is available at no charge on the GAO website at http://www.gao.gov.

If you or your staff have any questions about this report, please contact me at (202) 512-6806 or mihmj@gao.gov. Contact points for our Offices of Congressional Relations and Public Affairs may be found on the last page of this report. GAO staff who made major contributions to this report are listed in appendix IV.

J. Christopher Mihm
Managing Director, Strategic Issues

List of Committees

The Honorable Joseph I. Lieberman
Chairman
The Honorable Susan M. Collins
Ranking Member
Committee on Homeland Security and Governmental Affairs
United States Senate

The Honorable Patrick J. Leahy
Chairman
The Honorable Charles E. Grassley
Ranking Member
Committee on the Judiciary
United States Senate

The Honorable Charles E. Schumer
Chairman
The Honorable Lamar Alexander
Ranking Member
Committee on Rules and Administration
United States Senate

The Honorable Daniel E. Lungren
Chairman
The Honorable Robert A. Brady
Ranking Member
Committee on House Administration
House of Representatives

The Honorable Lamar S. Smith
Chairman
The Honorable John Conyers, Jr.
Ranking Member
Committee on the Judiciary
House of Representatives

The Honorable Darrell E. Issa
Chairman
The Honorable Elijah E. Cummings
Ranking Member
Committee on Oversight and Government Reform
House of Representatives

Appendix I: Objectives, Scope, and Methodology

Consistent with the audit mandates in the Honest Leadership and Open Government Act (HLOGA), our objectives were to

- determine the extent to which lobbyists are able to demonstrate compliance with the Lobbying Disclosure Act of 1995 as amended (LDA) by providing documentation to support information contained on registrations and reports filed under the LDA;
- identify any challenges to compliance and potential improvements; and
- describe the resources and authorities available to the U.S. Attorney's Office for the District of Columbia (the Office) and the efforts the Office has made to improve enforcement of the LDA, including identifying trends in past lobbying disclosure compliance.

To respond to our mandate, we used information in the lobbying disclosure database maintained by the Clerk of the House of Representatives (Clerk of the House). To assess whether these disclosure data were sufficiently reliable for the purposes of this report, we reviewed relevant documentation and spoke to officials responsible for maintaining the data. Although registrations and reports are filed through a single web portal, each chamber subsequently receives copies of the data and follows different data cleaning, processing, and editing procedures before storing the data in either individual files (in the House) or databases (in the Senate). Currently, there is no means of reconciling discrepancies between the two databases caused by the differences in data processing. For example, Senate staff have told us during previous reviews that they set aside a greater proportion of registration and report submissions than the House for manual review before entering the information into the database, and as a result, the Senate database would be slightly less current than the House database on any given day pending review and clearance. House staff also told us during previous reviews that they rely heavily on automated processing, and that while they manually review reports that do not perfectly match in formation file for a given registrant or client, they will approve and upload such reports as originally filed by each lobbyist even if the reports contain errors or discrepancies (such as a variant on how a name is spelled). Nevertheless, we do not have reasons to believe that the content of the Senate and House systems would vary substantially. For this review, we determined that House disclosure data were sufficiently reliable for identifying a sample of quarterly disclosure (LD-2) reports and for assessing whether newly filed registrants also filed required reports. We used the House database for sampling LD-2 reports from the third and fourth quarters of calendar year 2010 and the first and second quarters of

calendar year 2011, as well as for sampling year-end 2010 and midyear
2011 political contributions (LD-203) reports, and finally for matching
quarterly registrations with filed reports. We did not evaluate the Offices
of the Secretary of the Senate or the Clerk of the House, both of which
have key roles in the lobbying disclosure process, although we consulted
with officials from each office, and they provided us with general
background information at our request and detailed information on data
processing procedures.

To assess the extent to which lobbyists could provide evidence of their
compliance with reporting requirements, we examined a stratified random
sample of 100 LD-2 reports from the third and fourth quarters of 2010 and
the first and second quarters of 2011. The third quarter 2010 LD-2 reports
were from our prior review and were included in the current review to
redistribute the LD-2 reports evenly across the calendar year for future
lobbying reviews.[1] We excluded reports with no lobbying activity or with
income less than $5,000 from our sampling frame.[2] The third quarter
2010 sample was drawn from 13,489 activity reports and we drew our
remaining sample from 38,303 activity reports filed for the fourth quarter
of 2010 and first and second quarters of 2011 available in the public
House database, as of our final download date for each quarter. This
allowed us to generalize to a population of 51,792 activity reports. Our
sample is based on a stratified random selection, and it is only one of a
large number of samples that we may have drawn. Because each sample
could have provided different estimates, we express our confidence in the
precision of our particular sample's results as a 95 percent confidence
interval. This interval would contain the actual population value for 95
percent of the samples that we could have drawn. All percentage
estimates in this report have 95 percent confidence intervals of within plus
or minus 10.0 percentage points or less of the estimate itself, unless
otherwise noted. When estimating compliance with certain of the
elements we examined, we base our estimate on a one-sided 95 percent
confidence interval to generate a conservative estimate of either the

---

[1] For the prior review, we drew a stratified random sample of LD-2 reports from the fourth
quarter of 2009 and the first, second, and third quarters of 2010.

[2] LD-2 activity reports with "no lobbying issue activity" and reports with less than $5,000 in
reported income or expenses are filtered out because they do not contain verifiable
information on income, expenses, or activity.

minimum or the maximum percentage of reports in the population
exhibiting the characteristic.

We contacted all the lobbyists and lobbying firms in our sample and
asked them to provide support for key elements in their reports, including

- the amount of income reported for lobbying activities,
- the amount of expenses reported on lobbying activities,
- the names of those lobbyists listed in the report,
- the Houses of Congress and federal agencies that they lobbied, and
- the issue codes listed to describe their lobbying activity.

Prior to each interview, we conducted an open source search to identify
lobbyists on each report who may have held a covered official position.
We reviewed the lobbyists' previous work histories by searching lobbying
firms' websites, LinkedIn, Leadership Directories, Who's Who in American
Politics, Legistorm, and U.S. newspapers through Nexis. Prior to 2008,
lobbyists were only required to disclose covered official positions held
within 2 years of registering as a lobbyist for the client. HLOGA amended
that time frame to require disclosure of positions held 20 years before the
date the lobbyists first lobbied on behalf of the client. Lobbyist are
required to disclose previously held covered official positions either on the
client registration (LD-1) or on the first LD-2 report when the lobbyist is
added as "new." Consequently, those who held covered official positions
may have disclosed the information on the LD-1 or a LD-2 report filed
prior to the report we examined as part of our random sample. Therefore,
where we found evidence that a lobbyist previously held a covered official
position, we conducted an additional review of the publicly available
Secretary of the Senate or Clerk of the House database to determine
whether the lobbyist properly disclosed the covered official position.
Finally, if a lobbyist appeared to hold a covered position that was not
disclosed, we asked for an explanation at the interview with the lobbying
firm to ensure that our research was accurate. Despite our rigorous
search, it is possible that we failed to identify all previously held covered
official positions for all lobbyists listed. Thus, our estimate of the
proportion of reports with lobbyists who failed to properly disclose
covered official positions is a lower-bound estimate of the minimum
proportion of reports that failed to report such positions.

In addition to examining the content of the LD-2 reports, we confirmed
whether year-end 2010 or midyear 2011 LD-203 reports had been filed
for each firm and lobbyist listed on the LD-2 reports in our random
sample. Although this review represents a random selection of lobbyists

and firms, it is not a direct probability sample of firms filing LD-2 reports or lobbyists listed on LD-2 reports. As such, we did not estimate the likelihood that LD-203 reports were appropriately filed for the population of firms or lobbyists listed on LD-2 reports.

To determine if the LDA's requirement for registrants to file a report in the quarter of registration was met for the third and fourth quarters of 2010 and the first and second quarters of 2011, we used data filed with the Clerk of the House to match newly filed registrations with corresponding disclosure reports. Using direct matching and text and pattern matching procedures, we were able to identify matching disclosure reports for 3,357, or 88 percent, of the 3,802 newly filed registrations. We began by standardizing client and registrant names in both the report and registration files (including removing punctuation and standardizing words and abbreviations, such as "company" and "CO"). We then matched reports and registrations using the House identification number (which is linked to a unique registrant-client pair), as well as the names of the registrant and client. For reports we could not match by identification number and standardized name, we also attempted to match reports and registrations by client and registrant name, allowing for variations in the names to accommodate minor misspellings or typos. For these cases, we used professional judgment to determine whether cases with typos were sufficiently similar to consider as matches. We could not readily identify matches in the report database for the remaining registrations using electronic means.

To assess the accuracy of the LD-203 reports, we analyzed stratified random samples of LD-203 reports from the 32,301 total LD-203 reports. The first sample contains 80 reports of the 10,646 reports with political contributions and the second contains 80 reports of the 21,655 reports listing no contributions. Each sample contains 40 reports from the year-end 2010 filing period and 40 reports from the midyear 2011 filing period. The samples allow us to generalize estimates in this report to either the population of LD-203 reports with contributions or the reports without contributions to within a 95 percent confidence interval of plus or minus 8.2 percentage points or less, and to within 4.2 percentage points of estimate when analyzing both samples together. We analyzed the contents of the LD-203 reports and compared them to contribution data found in the publicly available Federal Elections Commission's (FEC) political contribution database. For our fiscal year 2009 report, we interviewed staff at the FEC responsible for administering the database and determined that the data reliability is suitable for the purpose of confirming whether a FEC-reportable disclosure listed in the FEC database had been reported on an LD-203 report.

We compared the FEC-reportable contributions reporting on the LD-203 reports with information in the FEC database. The verification process required text and pattern matching procedures, and we used professional judgment when assessing whether an individual listed is the same individual filing an LD-203. For contributions reported in the FEC database and not on the LD-203 report, we asked the lobbyists or organizations to provide an explanation of why the contribution was not listed on the LD-203 report or to provide documentation of those contributions. As with covered positions on LD-2 disclosure reports, we cannot be certain that our review identified all cases of FEC-reportable contributions that were inappropriately omitted from a lobbyist's LD-203 report. We did not estimate the percentage of other non-FEC political contributions that were omitted (such as honoraria or gifts to presidential libraries).

To identify challenges to compliance, we used structured interviews and obtained views from lobbyists included in our sample of LD-2 reports on any challenges to compliance. In addition, we asked lobbyists to rate various terms associated with disclosure requirements.

To describe the resources and authorities available to the Office, we interviewed officials from the Office and obtained information on the level of staffing and resources dedicated to the enforcement of the LDA. The Office provided us with information on the processes used to enforce compliance with the LDA, and reports from the tracking system on their number and status of referrals.

To describe the efforts the Office has made to improve its enforcement of the LDA, we interviewed officials from the Office and obtained information on the processes used by the Office in following up on referrals from the Secretary of the Senate and the Clerk of the House. The Office provided us with reports from the tracking system on the number and status of the referred cases.

The mandate does not include identifying lobbyists who failed to register and report in accordance with LDA requirements, or whether for those lobbyists who did register and report all lobbying activity or contributions were disclosed.

We conducted this performance audit from June 2011 through March
2012 in accordance with generally accepted government auditing
standards. Those standards require that we plan and perform the audit to
obtain sufficient, appropriate evidence to provide a reasonable basis for
our findings and conclusions based on our audit objectives. We believe
that the evidence obtained provides a reasonable basis for our findings
and conclusions based on our audit objectives.

Appendix II: List of Registrants and Clients for Sampled Lobbying Disclosure Reports

The random sample of lobbying disclosure reports we selected was based on unique combinations of registrant lobbyists and client names (see table 5).

Table 5: Names of Registrants and Clients Selected in Random Sample of Lobbying Disclosure Reports Filed in the Third and Fourth Quarters of 2010 and the First and Second Quarters of 2011

Registrant name	Client
Aguirre	The Geo Group Inc.
AJW, Inc.	Noresco
Akin Gump Strauss Hauer & Feld	Kohlberg Kravis Roberts & Company
Alcade & Fay	Marin County, California
American Continental Group	Liberty Lane Partners
American Gas Association	American Gas Association
American Network of Community Options & Resources	American Network of Community Options & Resources
Baker Donelson Bearman Caldwell & Berkowitz	Helen Keller National Center
Barbour Griffith & Rogers, LLC d/b/a BGR Government Affairs	The American Chamber of Commerce in the People's Republic of China (AmCham-China)
Barnes & Thornburg LLP	Town of Fishers
Behar & Kalman, LLP	National Association of Long Term Hospitals
Bockorny Group, Inc.	Elanco Animal Health
Brownstein Hyatt Farber Schreck, LLP	Z-MEDICA
Brownstein Hyatt Farber Schreck, LLP	Westwood College
Capitol Federal Strategies, LLC	GE Inspection Technologies
Capstone National Partners	Museum of Science and Industry
Cassidy & Associates, Inc. (formerly known as Cassidy & Associates)	Vion Corporation
Cavarocchi Ruscio Dennis Associates, L.L.C.	Coalition for Health Services Research
CG Technologies, Inc.	Dynetics, Inc.
Competition Advocates, LLC	Daikin Industries Limited
Concerned Women for America Legislative Action Committee	Concerned Women for America Legislative Action Committee
Cystic Fibrosis Foundation	Cystic Fibrosis Foundation
David Turch & Associates	City of Palmdale,
D.C. Legislative and Regulatory Services, Inc.	British Petroleum, America
DeBrunner & Associates, Inc.	Monongahela Valley Hospital
Defense Strategic Advantage, LLC	Sabreliner Corporation
Delta Strategy Group	Chesapeake Energy Corporation
Delta Strategy Group (formerly Parsons Strategies)	D.E. Shaw & Co., L.P.
Energy Future Holdings (formerly TXU Electric Delivery)	Energy Future Holdings (formerly TXU Electric Delivery)
Ernst & Young LLP (Washington Council Ernst & Young)	Covidien

Registrant name	Client
Etherton and Associates, Inc.	Lockheed Martin Corporation
Federal Policy Group (Clark & Wamberg LLC)	Cigar Association of America
Ferguson Group	Cary-NC, Town of
Firstenergy Corp	Firstenergy Corp
Fisher Consulting	Ball State University
Food Marketing Institute	Food Marketing Institute
Gephardt Group Government Affairs	Rational Entertainment Enterprises (on behalf of PokerStars)
Holland & Knight LLP	League of California Cities
Innovative Federal Strategies, LLC	Advatech Pacific, Inc.
JEH Government Services, Inc.	Appleton Paper
KAR Associates, LLC	Emergency Nurses Assn.
Law Offices of Kevin G. Curtin	Grocery Manufacturers/Food Products Association
Legislative Strategies, Inc.	Kinder Morgan CO2 Company LP
LeMunyon Group, LLC	Brazos River Authority
Liebman & Associates, Inc.	Lineage Power
Marlowe & Company	City of Havelock
Mattoon & Associates, LLC	Rolls-Royce North America, Inc.
Mayer Brown LLP	U.S. Chamber of Commerce
McAllister & Quinn LLC	Childhelp
mCapitol Management	Emergent Biosolutions
McGuireWoods Consulting	Dominion Resources, Inc.
McGuireWoods Consulting	Federal Home Loan Bank of Atlanta
ML Strategies, LLC	APCO Worldwide (Dow Corning)
Murray, Montgomery & O'Donnell	City of Phoenix
National Association of Credit Unions	National Association of Credit Unions
National Association of Letter Carriers	National Association of Letter Carriers
National Corn Growers Association	National Corn Growers Association
National Fair Housing Alliance	National Fair Housing Alliance
National Fisheries Institute	National Fisheries Institute
National Venture Capital Association	National Venture Capital Association
Navigators Global LLC (formerly DC Navigators, LLC)	Pala Band of Mission Indians
NCR Corporation	NCR Corporation
Nelson, Mullins, Riley & Scarborough	Maricopa County
New York Life Insurance Company	New York Life Insurance Company
North Shore Consultants	JASON Project
Ogilvy Government Relations	Ogilvy Public Relations on behalf of California High-Speed Rail

Registrant name	Client
Oglethorpe Power Corporation	Oglethorpe Power Corporation
Olsson Frank Weeda Terman Bode Matz PC	National Meat Association
O'Neill and Associates	Massachusetts Port Authority
Petrizzo Strategic Group, Inc.	Allen Institute for Brain Science
Podesta Group, Inc.	University of South Carolina
Public Strategies Washington	Anheuser-Busch Cos.
Quinn Gillespie & Associates	Satcon Technology Corporation
Quinn Gillespie & Associates	Cayman Finance
Ricchetti Incorporated	Novartis
Rose, Peter J.	Lockheed Martin Group
Russ Reid Company	Valparaiso University
Save Darfur Coalition	Save Darfur Coalition
Sears Holdings Corporation	Sears Holdings Corporation
Smith Dawson & Andrews	City of Fontana
SRG & Associates	Warren Corp.
Strafegies International, Ltd.	American Sesame Growers Association
Strategic Marketing Innovations	University of Maine
Strategic Marketing Innovations	Ingersoll Machine Tools
The Accord Group	Southern Company
The Glover Park Group LLC	Ernst & Young LLP
The Glover Park Group LLC	Amerilink Telecom Corporation
The Livingston Group, L.L.C.	New Orleans Business Council
The McManus Group	Genentech
The Nickles Group, LLC	Novartis Corporation
Troutman Sanders Public Affairs Group, LLC	City of Sacramento
Urban Swirski & Associates, LLC	National Association of Water Companies
Van Scoyoc Associates	The Rotary Foundation of Rotary International
Van Scoyoc Associates	City of Pismo Beach,
Van Scoyoc Associates	Martin County, Florida
White & Case LLP	Employee-Owned S Corporations of America
Whitmer & Worrall, LLC	Community College of Allegheny County
Williams & Jensen, PLLC	City of New Haven, Connecticut
Williams & Jensen, PLLC	U.S. Israel Science and Technology Foundation
Williams and Jensen, PLLC	County of Maui, Hawaii

Source: Lobbying disclosure database of the Clerk of the House of Representatives for the third and fourth quarters of calendar year 2010 and the first and second quarters of calendar year 2011.

Appendix III: List of Sampled Lobbying Contribution Reports with Contributions and No Contributions Listed

See table 6 for a list of lobbyists and lobbying firms from our random sample of lobbying contribution reports with contributions. See table 7 for a list of lobbyists and lobbying firms from our random sample of lobbying contribution reports without contributions.

Table 6: Lobbyists and Lobbying Firms in Random Sample of Lobbying Contribution Reports with Contributions Listed, Filed Year-end 2010 and Midyear 2011

Lobbyist or lobbying firm	Reporting period
Air Conditioning Contractors of America	Midyear 2011
Alan Slomowitz	Year-end 2010
American Resort Development Assn.	Midyear 2011
Association of Home Appliance Manufacturers	Year-end 2010
Baker Donelson Bearman Caldwell & Berkowitz	Year-end 2010
Business Software Alliance	Year-end 2010
Carl Chidlow	Year-end 2010
Cecil Swamidoss	Year-end 2010
Citigroup Management Corp.	Midyear 2011
Clothilde Hewlett	Midyear 2011
David Horne	Year-end 2010
David Polster	Midyear 2011
eBay Inc.	Midyear 2011
Edward Baxter	Year-end 2010
Elizabeth Sharp	Year-end 2010
Eric Stewart	Year-end 2010
Erin Martinko	Midyear 2011
Frederick Dombo	Midyear 2011
George Mannina	Midyear 2011
Grayson Winterling	Year-end 2010
Gregory Baise	Year-end 2010
Holcim (US) Inc.	Year-end 2010
James Gelfand	Year-end 2010
James Hooley	Midyear 2011
James Rock	Midyear 2011
Jeanne Campbell	Midyear 2011
John Blount	Midyear 2011
John Runyan	Midyear 2011
John Troy	Midyear 2011

Lobbyist or lobbying firm	Reporting period
Jose Fuentes	Year-end 2010
Josh Bourne	Year-end 2010
Kaiser Foundation Health Plan Inc.	Year-end 2010
Keith Amason	Year-end 2010
Kerry McKenney	Year-end 2010
Lawrence Pratt	Midyear 2011
Leann Fox	Year-end 2010
Leslie Belcher	Year-end 2010
Lisa Potetz	Year-end 2010
M. Skiles	Year-end 2010
Mark Disler	Year-end 2010
Mark Malone	Year-end 2010
Melinda Dutton	Year-end 2010
Melinda Maxfield	Midyear 2011
Michael Johnson	Year-end 2010
Michael Mawby	Midyear 2011
Michael Werner	Year-end 2010
Michelle Vogel	Year-end 2010
Mr. Jackson DeWitt	Year-end 2010
Mr. Robert Zimmer	Midyear 2011
Mrs. Helen Delich Bentley	Midyear 2011
National Air Traffic Controllers Association	Year-end 2010
National Association for Uniformed Services	Midyear 2011
National Association of Realtors	Midyear 2011
National Music Publishers' Association	Year-end 2010
Newmont Mining Corporation	Midyear 2011
Pablo Chavez	Year-end 2010
Patrick Carroll	Year-end 2010
Peter Loughlin	Midyear 2011
Peter Newbould	Midyear 2011
Public Service Enterprise Group	Midyear 2011
Richard Efford	Midyear 2011
Robert Hurt	Year-end 2010
Sandra Swirski	Midyear 2011
Scott Keefer	Year-end 2010
Scott Scanland	Midyear 2011
Sodexo Inc.	Year-end 2010

Lobbyist or lobbying firm	Reporting period
Steven Fisher	Midyear 2011
Steven McKnight	Midyear 2011
Susan Ingargiola	Year-end 2010
Ted Monoson	Midyear 2011
Terry Allen	Year-end 2010
Tesoro Companies	Midyear 2011
Thane Young	Midyear 2011
The GoodYear Tire & Rubber Company	Midyear 2011
Thomas Keating	Midyear 2011
Universal Music Group	Midyear 2011
Vicki Iseman	Midyear 2011
Vincent Versage	Midyear 2011
William Ris	Midyear 2011
Yahoo! Inc.	Year-end 2010

Source: Lobbying contributions database of the Clerk of the House of Representatives, Year-end reports for calendar year 2010 and midyear reports for calendar year 2011.

Table 7: Lobbyists and Lobbying Firms in Random Sample of Lobbying Contribution Reports with No Contributions Listed, Filed Year-end 2010 and Midyear 2011

Lobbyist or lobbying firm	Reporting period
Abby Bownas	Year-end 2010
Alan Ross	Year-end 2010
Alexis Latifi	Midyear 2011
Alliance for Excellent Education	Midyear 2011
American Business Conference	Midyear 2011
America's Blood Centers	Year-end 2010
Amy Edwards	Year-end 2010
Amy Rosenthal	Midyear 2011
Anne Duffy	Midyear 2011
BAFT-IFSA (formerly known as Bankers' Association for Finance & Trade)	Year-end 2010
Brendan Flanagan	Year-end 2010
Brigen Winters	Year-end 2010
Camille Donald	Midyear 2011
Capitol Counsel LLC	Midyear 2011

Lobbyist or lobbying firm	Reporting period
Charlene Macdonald	Year-end 2010
Christopher Kearney	Year-end 2010
Christopher Ross	Midyear 2011
Connect	Year-end 2010
Corporate Voices for Working Families	Midyear 2011
Craig Updyke	Year-end 2010
Daniel Smith	Year-end 2010
Darah Franklin	Midyear 2011
Darren Lasorte	Year-end 2010
Deirdre Stach	Year-end 2010
Dirk Vande Beek	Midyear 2011
Don Miller	Year-end 2010
Edward Edens	Year-end 2010
Edward Olivares	Midyear 2011
Emmer Consulting, P.C.	Midyear 2011
Fernando Gomez	Midyear 2011
Florida State University	Midyear 2011
Frank Ryan	Year-end 2010
Fred Searle	Midyear 2011
Geos Institute (formerly National Center for Conservation Sc)	Midyear 2011
Good Will Industries International Inc.	Year-end 2010
Harold Johnson	Midyear 2011
Heidi Salow	Midyear 2011
International Union of Operating Engineers	Midyear 2011
Jake Jacoby	Year-end 2010
James Kuhn	Year-end 2010
Jeffry P. Mahoney	Midyear 2011
Jerome Nagy	Year-end 2010
John Sabo	Year-end 2010
Jonathan Bergner	Midyear 2011
Joyce Knott	Midyear 2011
Kenneth Nahigian	Year-end 2010
Kevin Dempsey	Year-end 2010
Kirsten Zewers	Midyear 2011
Law Offices of James L. Kane, Jr.	Midyear 2011
Madison Government Affairs	Year-end 2010
Martin Regalia	Year-end 2010

Lobbyist or lobbying firm	Reporting period
Morgan Brown	Year-end 2010
Nancy Kohler	Midyear 2011
Natasha Bui	Year-end 2010
National Action Council for Minorities in Engineering, Inc.	Midyear 2011
National Alliance on Mental Illness	Midyear 2011
Nora Super	Midyear 2011
Patricia Chavez	Year-end 2010
Porter Delaney	Midyear 2011
Priscilla Chatman	Year-end 2010
Profit Sharing/401(K) Council of America	Midyear 2011
Rachel Hedge	Midyear 2011
Rebecca Kelly	Midyear 2011
Redfern Resources	Year-end 2010
Ryan Quinn	Midyear 2011
Safety Net Hospitals for Pharmaceutical Access	Midyear 2011
Scott North	Year-end 2010
Scott Thompson	Midyear 2011
Sean Heather	Year-end 2010
Stephan Bell	Year-end 2010
Steve Gotthiem	Year-end 2010
Steven Brownlee	Midyear 2011
Terry Francl	Year-end 2010
The Collette Group LLC	Midyear 2011
Traditional Values Coalition	Midyear 2011
Washington University in St. Louis	Year-end 2010
Wayne LaPierre	Year-end 2010
William Cloherty	Midyear 2011
William Weber	Year-end 2010
Yvonne Roberts	Year-end 2010

Source: Lobbying contributions database of the Clerk of the House of Representatives, Year-end reports for calendar year 2010 and midyear reports for calendar year 2011.

Appendix IV: GAO Contact and Staff Acknowledgments

GAO Contact	J. Christopher Mihm, (202) 512-6806 or mihmj@gao.gov
Staff Acknowledgments	In addition to the contact named above, Robert Cramer, Associate General Counsel; Bill Reinsberg, Assistant Director; Shirley Jones, Assistant General Counsel; Crystal Bernard; Amy Bowser; Colleen Candrl; Jill Lacey; Natalie Maddox; Donna Miller; Anna Maria Ortiz; Melanie Papasian; and Katrina Taylor made key contributions to this report. Assisting with lobbyist file reviews were Vida Awumey, Alexandra Edwards, Emily Gruenwald, Lois Hanshaw, Jeff McDermott, Stacey Ann Spence, Megan Taylor and Daniel Webb.

GAO's Mission	The Government Accountability Office, the audit, evaluation, and investigative arm of Congress, exists to support Congress in meeting its constitutional responsibilities and to help improve the performance and accountability of the federal government for the American people. GAO examines the use of public funds; evaluates federal programs and policies; and provides analyses, recommendations, and other assistance to help Congress make informed oversight, policy, and funding decisions. GAO's commitment to good government is reflected in its core values of accountability, integrity, and reliability.
Obtaining Copies of GAO Reports and Testimony	The fastest and easiest way to obtain copies of GAO documents at no cost is through GAO's website (www.gao.gov). Each weekday afternoon, GAO posts on its website newly released reports, testimony, and correspondence. To have GAO e-mail you a list of newly posted products, go to www.gao.gov and select "E-mail Updates."
Order by Phone	The price of each GAO publication reflects GAO's actual cost of production and distribution and depends on the number of pages in the publication and whether the publication is printed in color or black and white. Pricing and ordering information is posted on GAO's website, http://www.gao.gov/ordering.htm. Place orders by calling (202) 512-6000, toll free (866) 801-7077, or TDD (202) 512-2537. Orders may be paid for using American Express, Discover Card, MasterCard, Visa, check, or money order. Call for additional information.
Connect with GAO	Connect with GAO on Facebook, Flickr, Twitter, and YouTube. Subscribe to our RSS Feeds or E-mail Updates. Listen to our Podcasts. Visit GAO on the web at www.gao.gov.
To Report Fraud, Waste, and Abuse in Federal Programs	Contact: Website: www.gao.gov/fraudnet/fraudnet.htm E-mail: fraudnet@gao.gov Automated answering system: (800) 424-5454 or (202) 512-7470
Congressional Relations	Katherine Siggerud, Managing Director, siggerudk@gao.gov, (202) 512-4400, U.S. Government Accountability Office, 441 G Street NW, Room 7125, Washington, DC 20548
Public Affairs	Chuck Young, Managing Director, youngc1@gao.gov, (202) 512-4800 U.S. Government Accountability Office, 441 G Street NW, Room 7149 Washington, DC 20548